Izabel Soares de Lima Huning

The rancour and progress of inclusive education for human rights

Izabel Soares de Lima Huning

The rancour and progress of inclusive education for human rights

What is the teacher's role in mediating learning?

ScienciaScripts

Imprint

Any brand names and product names mentioned in this book are subject to trademark, brand or patent protection and are trademarks or registered trademarks of their respective holders. The use of brand names, product names, common names, trade names, product descriptions etc. even without a particular marking in this work is in no way to be construed to mean that such names may be regarded as unrestricted in respect of trademark and brand protection legislation and could thus be used by anyone.

Cover image: www.ingimage.com

This book is a translation from the original published under ISBN 978-3-330-76344-9.

Publisher:
Sciencia Scripts
is a trademark of
Dodo Books Indian Ocean Ltd. and OmniScriptum S.R.L publishing group

120 High Road, East Finchley, London, N2 9ED, United Kingdom
Str. Armeneasca 28/1, office 1, Chisinau MD-2012, Republic of Moldova, Europe
Printed at: see last page
ISBN: 978-620-8-08953-5

THE ACHIEVEMENTS AND PROGRESS OF INCLUSIVE EDUCATION FOR HUMAN RIGHTS

Izabel Soares de Lima Huning[I]

Summary

Thinking about inclusive education leads us to review the concepts of what inclusion is, in order to understand being and being in society, and how it has been produced and reproduced for centuries. In this sense, it is essential to talk about and act on inclusion, demystifying misconceptions that the target audience of inclusive education is not capable of producing knowledge. Therefore, thinking about inclusion for the realization of human rights means re-signifying the concepts of inclusion, extending its understanding to all levels of education. The aim of this work is to generate reflections and questions about the importance of training the subject to exercise citizenship, by giving this target group a differentiated and egalitarian look. Our aim is to promote reflection on inclusive education for the exercise of human rights, making it possible to understand its importance at all levels of education. Therefore, inclusion presupposes the act of educating and/or teaching children, adolescents, young people and adults together, understanding the social and cultural relationships that already exist. In this analysis, the most important thing is to understand the function of the Zone of Proximal Development and, based on this, to create intervention strategies between teacher and student, as new paths emerge that make it possible to expand their cognitive capacities.

Keywords: Human Rights; Inclusion; Valorization.

[I] Degree in Geography and Special Education and Specialist in Education, Human Rights and Diversities from the Community University of the Region of Chapeco; Teacher in the State Public network of the State of Santa Catarina, Email- izabelhuning@gmail.com or izabelhuning@unochapeco.edu.br

Summary

Chapter 1	3
Chapter 2	5
Chapter 3	40
Chapter 4	42

1 Introduction

Thinking about inclusive education leads us to review the concepts of what inclusion/integration is, in the sense of understanding what it means to be and to be in society, and how it has been produced and reproduced for centuries, as well as the model of man that we want to build, In this sense, it is essential to speak and act in order to understand the process of inclusion/integration, demystifying the distorted ideas that the target audience of inclusive education is not capable of producing knowledge based on the interpretation of concepts.

Therefore, when we think about inclusion for the realization of human rights, it means giving a new meaning to the concepts of inclusion, extending its understanding to all levels of education. The aim of this work is to generate reflections and questions about the importance of training the subject to exercise citizenship, taking a differentiated and egalitarian look at the target public of inclusive education, demystifying the idea that it only encompasses students with special needs.

The aim is to achieve results based on the assimilation of new concepts of the importance of the theme of inclusion for human rights, guided by the importance of pedagogical practices that provide opportunities for the production of knowledge based on the possibility of re-signifying the concepts of what inclusion is and what it is for.

There is an urgent need to understand the importance of inclusion for human rights, emphasizing the real importance of these rights for the effective exercise of citizenship. To do this, it is important to look at their life stories, because it is clear that human rights education is being thought of through the social relationships that the target audience of inclusive education has in today's society.

So reflecting on history implies undoing a customary stereotype that for centuries made some social groups invisible, or even those who had learning difficulties of all kinds and therefore had to be separated from the rest because they were considered incapable of interacting with others in the same space.

That's why inclusive education calls into question educational practices that aim to deepen the individualism of both teachers and students. To this end, it changes the traditional structure, whether it's the training of education professionals or the organization of teaching levels, making teachers mobilize in order to develop diversified methodologies that result in learning, This is because inclusive education is very broad and in order to meet it, professionals must establish rules for re-signifying what it means to be and what it means to want, thus recognizing their intelligence and always valuing them in relation to the environment in which they are inserted throughout their training in human rights.

To do this, it can and should use methods that establish references and meanings for the subjects of inclusive education, taking their experiences into account.

Our aim is to promote reflections on inclusive education for the exercise of human rights, making it possible to understand its importance at all levels of education. It is true that it is not presented in a finished form, but as part of a process that is built day by day, because inclusion is formed taking into account the lived history of the subjects who make up the target audience of inclusive education.

2 WHAT IS THE ROLE OF THE TEACHER IN MEDIATING LEARNING?

Any process of inclusion requires first and foremost an understanding of the meaning of integration, given that this is a process that requires the participation of all those involved in the context, where relationships are preponderant insofar as they determine the relationships between the social groups involved, so interaction requires a reciprocity between the act of including and integrating in human rights, so teaching spaces and teaching staff must adopt differentiated strategies according to the needs and abilities presented by the groups.

Inclusion for rights therefore presupposes the act of educating and/or teaching children, adolescents, young people and adults together, understanding the social and cultural relationships that are taking place. It is important to emphasize that this is a complex and gradual process, which in turn varies according to the characteristics of the group, but the conditions of the environment in which these relationships take place must also be taken into account.

From this perspective, inclusion for human rights needs to be taken up by all those involved at all levels of education, so that it is no longer the exclusive goal of those qualified to carry out this function, but requires changes in attitudes towards the social and cultural differences present in the group, This implies adopting attitudes of non-rejection, otherwise we run the risk of merely including them in the educational levels to the extent that we provide the subjects with the necessary conditions for the realization of socio-spatial relations in a new historical context.

Thinking about inclusion for human rights raises a series of discussions about the difficulties that these groups have faced throughout history, a fact that represents a major challenge for the teachers involved in the process of making them take ownership of knowledge and how to do things, tools that are indispensable for exercising future citizenship.

It is therefore necessary to promote a series of changes in the organizational structure of pedagogical proposals, so that the needs of each culture can be simultaneously recognized and valued, without discriminating against them, while at the same time seeking to include them without segregating any of the students in the group, bearing in mind that the process of inclusion is a double-edged sword, where Carvalho apud Demo (1999, p.37-38) points out that;

> "The inclusive school, that is, the school for all, must be part of an inclusive world where inequalities - which are structural in societies - do not reach levels as high as those we have experienced", of segregation of minorities throughout history.

Thus, *"enforcing the right to education for all is not limited to complying with the law and summarily applying it to discriminatory situations"* (MANTOAN E PRIETO, 2006 p.16).), but to understand what the process is and why it should be understood in its entirety, because thinking about inclusion for human rights requires a new look at the process of learning for all, where inclusion represents nothing more than the interaction of all subjects and their peculiarities, thus *"being people is always running the risk of being different"* (MANTOAN AND PRIETO, 2006 p.17).

It is important to emphasize that the process of inclusion for human rights needs to be detached from the segregational process offered to subjects and their cultures, as an integral part of the teaching-learning process, because there are different ways of understanding who these subjects are and that they can be offered tools to understand the importance of being included in all levels of education without being served in a parallel structure, as Wallon (2010, p.52) points out;

> The [...] does not occur from bifurcation to bifurcation by distinct units, but as an outline of the whole, remanaged from attempt to attempt. It is from the qualitative succession that the units emerge in succession, and not from units that are simply juxtaposed, that learning the correct path results.

In other words, inclusion for human rights requires a joint effort to be developed at all levels of education, but without promoting the distancing of those involved and pedagogical strategies aimed at inclusive practices in their entirety, because, *"Directions and distances merge into a kind of dynamic whole whose search guides the animal. The effect is not external to the act. It is at all times simultaneously its result and its regulator."* WALLON (2010, p. 52)

From this perspective, education cannot be organized in parallel structures; rather, inclusion in human rights takes place in the context of socio-spatial relations, but whenever the need for inclusion is identified, it must be understood and defined by public policies.

In the current socio-historical context, there is no possibility of a return to the segregation of yesteryear. However, adjustments need to be made to teaching methods that make it possible to understand and assimilate the importance of being in space and of learning and knowing how to learn, which will result in inclusion and learning itself.

As described by Carbonari (2011 p.04), political action would be centered on the presence of all agents, both in deliberation and implementation, as subjects (authors, therefore, never just actors). This means that citizenship in general, and especially active and organized citizenship, takes on a fundamental centrality in the political process.

In general, when we talk about inclusion for human rights, it is worth remembering that we are always led to think of everyone in a homogeneous way, even though society is heterogeneous par excellence, and this automatically creates an understanding that "equality of opportunity is perverse when it guarantees access, for example, to ordinary schools for people who do not have the same chance as others due to problems beyond their control" (MANTOAN and PRIETO, 2006).

This fact requires assistance that provides support to overcome the obstacles that present themselves in its extension, so the levels of education must be anchored in the strategic support that is available from public policies, It is up to the professionals who will work at these levels to be prepared and imbued with methodologies that meet the needs of all this target public, overcoming all the limitations that come with it. Thus, *"equality is not a goal to be achieved, but a starting point, an assumption to be maintained in all circumstances".(MANTOAN* and PRIETO, 2006, p.21).

It is worth noting that inclusion for human rights has been organized and structured with the aim of providing access to education for all those who present some socio-historical characteristic peculiar to their origin, to the extent that at all levels of education, professionals can develop working methods that aim to cater for all cultures, creeds and needs, ranging from physical disabilities to typical behaviours or high abilities, creeds and needs, ranging from physical disabilities, intellectual disabilities, typical behaviors or high abilities, with the aim of integrating them into the levels of education, because this aims to provide care that provides the exercise of citizenship or even an additional contribution to the learning process itself, because to

Wallon (2010, p 71-72),

> [...] at the same time as their differentiation is accentuated, the field of excitation is broadened and refined. The elementary excitation gives way to a whole that makes its meaning more precise; these can be current impressions but also the traces of previous impressions and behaviors.

Inclusion for human rights thus aims to reverse the segregational situation in education systems, where the right to education was restricted to those who were visible and it was up to the group considered invisible to stay away from these spaces open to a few, a fact that was accentuated with regard to pupils with special needs, in order to reverse this paradox in the right to be and to be in school.

And from this perspective, inclusion for human rights becomes fundamental to understanding the process of inclusion of this group, as well as the way in which teaching-learning is processed in an inter- and transdisciplinary way, including them and not just integrating them into the levels of education, bearing in mind that in these spaces the subject comes into contact with diversified methods that provide them with a better understanding of the exercise of citizenship, which as a rule is processed from knowledge.

For Wallon (2010, p.155), Through language, the object of thought ceases to be exclusively that which, because of its presence, imposes itself on perception. It gives the representation of things that no longer exist or could exist the means to be evoked, confronted with each other and with what is felt now.

Wallon (2010, p. 157) adds,

> The designation of time and its precise identification undoubtedly require a sliding of the three terms: tomorrow, today, yesterday, successively in the same sentence, and the relativity of this adjustment between words and things presupposes an unfolding of planes on which the objects of thought are projected that is already of a high mental evolution.

It is important to highlight that in this new scenario, inclusion for human rights must be guided by the observation of previously acquired skills, for the subsequent application of new processes aimed at the development and acquisition of new skills, so inclusion helps in the construction of knowledge and skills, of all participants in the organization of knowledge to the extent that there is construction and feeding in the cognitive assimilation of knowledge.

There is the possibility of organizing new pedagogical apparatuses that aim to eliminate the barriers to the exclusion of these subjects from the levels of education, making it possible for everyone to participate better, but these activities must not take on the character of a substitute for their historical cultures, but rather develop capacities that aim to enrich the curricular presuppositions, where Wallon (2010, p;161) points out that,

> Syncretism produces very similar effects. It is a kind of compromise, on various levels, between the representation sought and the moving complexity of experience. To define it, it is best to compare it with the essential distinctions on which adult thought rests.

In this analysis, it seems pertinent to paraphrase Vygotsky, because using the Zone of Proximal Development means creating intervention strategies between teacher and student, to the extent that new paths emerge that make it possible to expand their cognitive capacities and this, in turn, becomes the appropriation of knowledge, as is also advocated by other theories such as constructivism and social interactionism, which emphasize the need to make the invisible visible, hence the importance of valuing the historical and cultural background of all subjects who are the target of inclusive education.

It is from this perspective that educators such as Paulo Freire and others understand that inclusion can create more authentic mechanisms with regard to the subject, which means an advance on their right to exercise their citizenship, where inclusive education will become effective as a result of a sum of opportunities offered to all, including all cultures, creeds or students with special needs.

It's an attitude that leads us to accept differences as a whole, but actually including them goes beyond simply putting one more student in the classroom; we need to integrate them and make them feel like subjects of an incredibly dualistic and fragmented society.

The process of inclusion then provides for the participation of all at all levels of education, safeguarding the right to Specialized Educational Assistance for all children with learning difficulties, where access to education is the right of all and provided for by law, but it has to be offered in a flexible way so that students succeed in exercising their citizenship, in other words, it is necessary for this target audience to become visible based on the immediate adjustments proposed by educators.

For real inclusion, spaces need to consider their daily lives, taking into account the needs and abilities of the subjects, their cultures and the values that will guide pedagogical practice.

It is true that this presupposes the immediate adaptation of teaching curricula, where necessary, to make it appropriate to the peculiarities of the students, i.e. there is no need to organize a new legal curriculum for basic education.

However, the education professional needs to make the curriculum dynamic, changeable and expandable, so that it effectively caters for all these students, so that they succeed in understanding the concepts taught there, and this understanding must be extended to their practical lives.

The aim of curriculum adaptation is therefore to make the invisible visible, in other words, to bring the curriculum closer to the conditions of the subject's peculiarities in the classroom, because the act of adapting needs to promote immediate adjustments in the way the pedagogical process is carried out, and thereby promote the appreciation of the subject (man: world-sphere) who is in constant articulation with his peers.

In other words, their invisibility is no longer conceivable, since the school must promote the act of educating for coexistence insofar as it promotes and/or praises the importance of the self and the other.

This is nothing more than creating in the school environment respect and understanding of the otherness of the self and the other, a fundamental element for the realization of inclusion for human rights, these are the existing ranks with regard to their realization, because there is still a lot to be done for this historical process to be effective.

On the other hand, it's well known that this won't happen overnight, given that it's necessary to know how to do it, especially in days when the teacher himself is at a fork in the road, trying to find his Self and at the same time having to deal with a wide range of diversity, as Santos (1988, p.164) points out,

> ... we live in a time of porosity and, therefore, of ethical and legal porosity, of a porous law made up of multiple networks of legal orders that force us into constant transitions and transgressions. Socio-legal life at the end of the [20th] century is made up of the intersection of different border lines and respect for some necessarily implies the violation of others. The intersection of ethical and

From this perspective, it is important for teachers to think about curricular adaptations for the realization of human rights in order to cross the boundaries between being and being in the school space. In this way, a rich inter- and trans-disciplinary approach can be implemented in order to provide the real conditions to make visible the group that has been invisible from obtaining knowledge and learning in all the relationships that are eminent to the subject's life and culture at school and beyond.

Curricular adjustments must take into account the subject (the concrete diversity) of the classroom, but the teacher himself cannot shirk the role of also transforming himself in view of the fact that there needs to be a global transformation in his surroundings, because the school today is not the same as it was in the last century, and for this reason there is a need to overcome the very human needs that will strengthen the realization of inclusion for human rights.

In this sense, promoting adaptations does not mean using what already exists in national curricula, but rather renewing and/or making immediate adjustments to their structure, spreading the possibilities of using new pedagogical concepts in a more humanitarian way and, in turn, making it possible to revitalize pedagogical practice based on new ways of thinking about scientific and philosophical concepts, so that everyone is able to appropriate the knowledge already produced from the zone of proximal development.

It is worth remembering that the learning process of a person with special needs requires immediate modifications or adjustments in the process of making the pedagogical application, so to speak, and these supports must begin with the teacher's practice of promoting the Curricular Adaptations necessary for teaching and learning.

All adjustments and modifications made to the different curricular levels must respond to the needs of each student, always safeguarding the individual conditions necessary for learning to take place as much as possible.

Curricular Adaptations are supports that should promote the conditions necessary for the learning of each included student, because they have special educational needs, regardless of their physical, cultural or cognitive conditions, so they need supports that favor their access to knowledge and its functional use, in the management of their own lives, and in the process of transforming society, and this is achieved through curricular adaptations.

In this way, curriculum adaptation for students who are the target of inclusive education becomes a right, and is provided for in the National Education Guidelines and Bases Law - LDBEN, Law No. 9.394 (BRASIL, 1996), and in some materials and documents issued by government bodies, among them: the National Curriculum Parameters: Curricular Adaptations - Strategies for the Education of Students with Special Educational Needs (BRASIL, 1998) and the Living School Project which maintains: Guaranteeing access and permanence for all students at school - Students with special needs (BRASIL, 2000a; 2000b).

It can also be found in Decree No. 3.298, which governs the National Policy for the Integration of People with Disabilities (BRASIL, 1999c), in the National Guidelines for Special Education in Basic Education (BRASIL, 2001f), in the Document Subsidizing the Inclusion Policy (BRASIL, 2005), in the Educational Policy for Special Education from the Perspective of Inclusive Education (BRASIL, 2008a) and in CNE/CEB Resolution No. 4 of October 2, which establishes Guidelines for Specialized Educational Assistance in Basic Education (BRASIL, 2009b).

It is important to point out that adjustments in support for the care of the group belonging to inclusive education, such as people with special needs, have been breathing down our necks since the mid-1990s, such as the curricular adaptation provided for in the Salamanca Declaration (UNESCO, 1994) in Article 26, which deals with school-related factors, ensuring that *the curriculum must be adapted to the specific needs of the student and not the other way around*. To this end, it is necessary to take into account that each student has different abilities and interests, and that the school must offer appropriate curricular opportunities.

Despite the use of the term curricular adequacy, it was noted that historiography also uses the terms curricular adaptation and curricular flexibilization, but we will stick to the term adequacy because we understand that it comprises a set of immediate actions promoted by teachers in order to provide teaching and learning opportunities for students with disabilities, in other words, it alludes to the importance of curricular adjustments for students, because they are;

It is important to point out that, based on official documents such as the National Curriculum Parameters: Curricular Adaptations/Adadequacies: are Strategies for the Education of Students with Special Educational Needs, and establish that curricular actions should consider [...] *what the student should learn; how and when to learn; what forms of teaching organization are most efficient for the learning process; how and when to evaluate the student"* *(BRASIL, 1998, p. 33).*

In other words, it is possible to see that Brazilian educational policies over the last few decades have been based on inclusive discourses, in the wake of the universalization of basic education. However, in order for this to be effective, there is a lot to be done, although these discourses are gaining strength within civil society, as it is an issue that keeps alive the important links with funding institutions for the maintenance of contracts between international agencies and national governments.(MICHELLIS & GARCIA 2010, p 212)

It is worth remembering that when organizing actions to guarantee human rights in pedagogical work from special education to basic education, the teacher must rely on two currents.

The first is the current of homogenizing education, taking on and supporting all the criticism that comes its way, defending the need and importance of special education for this target group.

The second current that this group of teachers must adhere to is that special education must be recognized as a right, and in order to do so, they need to make use of all the mechanisms they have to ensure that these students no longer form part of the heterogeneity of basic education and no longer remain on the margins of mainstream education, but form part of a homogeneous group, the much-dreamed-of equality for all, this is the great bottleneck to be overcome by special education professionals.

In order for these currents to take hold, other obstacles have to be overcome, such as the debates around teachers' pedagogical positions, where and how the specialized educational service will take place, the role of special education in basic education and the importance of making curricula more flexible for this target public, given that the teacher training process is still not geared towards guaranteeing human rights in their entirety, given that this is done in a fragmented way and by specificity along the lines of the last century.

Pedagogical actions aimed at education to guarantee human rights are limited to special education, which is why they have a "[...] *curricular dimension that is essential for the planning and practice of schooling processes for people with disabilities"* (MAGALHAES, 2012, p. 493).

That's why all the challenges related to curricular adaptations began when the Secretariat for Special Education (MEC/SEESP) published the document Parametros Curriculares Nacionais: Adaptagoes Curriculares: Strategies for the Education of Students with Special Educational Needs in 1998. This document helped pedagogical practice by proposing adaptations in objectives, content, and also in the evaluation process, with temporality, corroborating with the organization of didactic-pedagogical work and also helping in the teaching-learning process (BRASIL, 1998).

It is worth noting that Brazil is following the international trend by adopting the term "curricular adaptation" in its special education policies in order to name all the pedagogical actions intended to adapt the curriculum and thus provide educational responses to the needs of students in the school context (HEREDERO, 2010).

However, when we refer to the existing ranges in the process of inclusion for human rights, we are thinking of the immediate adjustments made by teachers to meet the specific needs of the target audience of inclusive education, bearing in mind that these adjustments must take into account the abilities and skills of the group presented to them.

As a result, on April 4, 2013, in the light of Law No.º 12.796, in its article 59, there was an amendment to LDBN 9394/96, in which the need for adaptations for the care of students with disabilities, global development disorders and high abilities or giftedness *"specific curricula, methods, techniques, educational resources and organization"* to meet their needs regardless of cultural conditions is evident.

Art. 26 of the same law states that the curricula of basic education, regardless of level, must be "[...] *complemented, in each education system and in each school, by a diversified part, required by the regional and local characteristics of society, culture, economy and students"* (BRASIL, 2013, p.2).), in other words, students are guaranteed the right to curricular adaptation and it is up to the teacher to promote these actions, for which they need to receive adequate training, which is also a right guaranteed by the new education policy.

In the same vein, many other authors have highlighted the importance of making curricula more flexible so that the teaching-learning process of the included person is effective, because the school is the space where the act of mediating takes place, and for this reason it needs to be as democratic as possible, as highlighted by Apud, Mello 1991 (MAZZOTA, 2011.p.136).

> ...functions of a different nature may be taken on by the school institution, due to the imposition of historical and social contingencies, but they must be subordinated to the fundamental task of managing the pedagogical relationship through which teaching and learning take place.

In this way, if we think about the process of inclusion for the realization of human rights, despite the role of the school and its actors, in assuming the role of making education the dimension of homogenizing the right to be and to be in space, the true sense of what education for human rights is, This is becoming more widespread and easier to accept, whether on the part of the mainstream teacher or on the part of the student who is considered normal. However, in order for this to happen, adjustments need to be made to the way the teaching-learning process is mediated.

This is because in order to work with human rights education, we first need to strengthen a culture of respect, based on the objective and effectiveness of values and the principle of human dignity. The challenges of inclusion lie in providing opportunities for cultural and democratic coexistence, which strives for equality and cultural formation.

Curriculum adaptation and its legal bases guided by human rights: where are the gaps in inclusion?

In order to make the right to inclusion a reality and guarantee it, we need to think about the pedagogical approaches presented by the historiography of the education of people who are the target of special education and, ultimately, think based on the practical attempts made by the social movements they themselves created to overcome segregation and "overcome the challenges they face in different times and places" (JANUZZI, 2012, p.25).

With a view to the right to equality for people with disabilities, this is fundamental to protecting their right to human otherness, undoing the idea that this public belonged to the group in which the right was fourth generation and therefore sums up the future of citizenship and the future of these same people, creating and maintaining the basic assumptions of a life in freedom and human dignity.

Complemented by Salvat (Apud MAGENDZO, 1994, p.164):

> Human rights appear to us as a utopia to be promoted and shaped by different levels and spheres of society. As such, they are presented as an ethical-political framework that serves as criticism and guidance (real and symbolic) in relation to the different social practices (legal, economic, educational, etc.) in the never-ending struggle for a fairer and freer social order. In this sense, they are seen as paradigmatic, that is, as an exemplary model and/or criterion from which we can read our history and our future as peoples.

In other words, society in general has undergone significant transformations and the population is aware of this, but this same society has not yet become aware that it is necessary to make the invisible visible, because they are not yet understood as citizens by right and therefore require ways of understanding the individual and the changes they bring about in all areas of society.

It is important to point out that, since the right to social inclusion is a designation of the right to otherness of the disabled person, this is, in turn, as Bonavides (2000, p. 3) points out:

> [...] the governing principle of second generation fundamental rights, consisting of social, cultural and economic rights. Considering that the inclusion of people with disabilities aims to preserve equality, the right to social inclusion of people with disabilities is also part of the second dimension of fundamental rights.

From this perspective, to the extent that civil society comes to understand and accept that special education is part of the process of making visible the part of the population that has remained invisible for centuries, it also becomes *"the function of school education, to be better understood and explained by and for society (civil and political), the understanding of common or regular education and special education will become clearer and more generalizing"* (MAZZOTTA 2011, p.136).), for a better understanding of the sense and meaning of the importance of making the invisible visible in the face of a society that was formed in an exclusionary way.

It is worth emphasizing that awareness of the challenges and struggles for an education geared towards human rights and these struggles are reflected in support aimed at improving the lives of people with disabilities as they fight for inclusion to become a reality through thoughtful practice that suggests the social interventions needed to make the know-how a reality.

Bearing in mind that every action suggests a reaction, or as (MAGENDZO, 1994) points out, "the meaning of an action is given by the meaning of others, which follow and so on". Therefore, if we look at the meaning of the concept of human rights in historiography, we realize that it has been built up based on the historical structures of its own human evolution, which is why linearity becomes indispensable.

Therefore, it is up to the school to search for answers within the educational process adjusted by the teachers to meet the needs of their students with the aim of valuing and safeguarding their differences and providing a better quality of education for all.

In the historiography of Special Education in the Perspective of Inclusive Education, we find in the guiding assumptions of the National Special Education Policy, with regard to Inclusive Education, the guidelines of access for all, guaranteeing the right to participation and learning regardless of their physical or cognitive conditions:

> Transversality of special education from early childhood education to higher education; Specialized educational care; Continuity of schooling at higher levels of education; Training of teachers for specialized educational care and other education professionals for school inclusion; Participation of the family and the community; Accessibility in urban, architectural, furniture and equipment, transport, communication and information; and articulation in the implementation of public policies. (BRASIL 2010)

In another analysis, we can point out that when we refer to inclusion, we are not referring to the gender-species relationship, because this in itself is part of fundamental rights, which are the human rights enshrined in the text of the Federal Constitution, and it is therefore up to society to ensure that they participate in all segments, including education, and this is one of the challenges that society needs to overcome, because if the law takes steps towards making them visible, there are obstacles at school that still make them invisible.

From this perspective, human rights appear truncated, since they do not establish the link between being and being in space, that is, between the part and the whole, or rather, whenever the concept of human rights is centered on what is simply derivative, the rights, instead of focusing on the primordial imperative, in this case that of making the invisible visible, so that individuals, regardless of their condition, can find their place in the general order of society.

The problems are many, but the school needs to adapt to the needs of students, regardless of their physical, cultural or cognitive conditions, and ongoing training can provide support so that teachers can develop their pedagogical practice with a commitment to giving students with disabilities access to the knowledge they are working on. In this direction, the adaptation of materials, resources and the immediate adaptation of curricula, according to the student's needs, becomes fundamental.

HOBSBAWM 1995 (Apud Januzzi 2012, p.141) points to this line of thinking:

> [...] at the end of the 20th century, the individual triumphed over society, and there was a certain break in the social texture. Previously, this texture was expressed not only in the actual relationships between people, but also in the way they organized themselves, in the expected patterns of behaviour between them.

Complemented by article 24 of the Special Education Policy (Brazil 2010)

> a) people with disabilities are not excluded from the general education system on the grounds of disability and that children with disabilities are not excluded from compulsory free primary education on the grounds of disability; b) people with disabilities can access inclusive, quality, free primary education on equal terms with others in the community in which they live.

The challenges of inclusion for the realization of human rights lie in the fact that "it is in the heart of society that man develops" (Januzzi 2012 p.26), so in order to make the invisible visible through the process of inclusion, it also points to the improvement of schools, be it in relation to teachers, who will direct their actions towards the subjects they serve. To this end, it is worth bearing in mind:

> [...] their own creations to overcome the challenges they face - **we are talking here about the teacher (my emphasis)** in different times and places; through observation and the daily efforts of people who are committed to helping them

survive, and also through the application of knowledge gained from the various sciences. (JANUZZI 2012 p.25)

From this perspective, the differences to be considered in the process of inclusion cannot be evaluated as a problem or obstacle to be overcome, but rather as a mechanism that will richly assist us in the process of making learning possible for everyone, regardless of their physical, cultural or cognitive conditions. This is because inclusion is linked to the reciprocal efforts of the relationship between schools and their communities.

The process of inclusion has been gaining momentum in the debates surrounding basic education throughout the country, taking into account the principle of equal conditions for access and permanence for everyone in school, regardless of their condition. However, these are the challenges that we are still seeing at the dawn of the 21st century, because in order for inclusion to be fully realized, the process itself has been suggesting a reversal of the old paradigms and concepts of normality and standards of learning, has been suggesting that the old paradigms and concepts of normality and standards of learning mediation should be reversed, in order to establish new values in the school that contemplate citizenship, thus guaranteeing universal access and ensuring the right in the different spheres of the social structure (SANTOS, 1997).

It is worth remembering that the aim of inclusion is to integrate everyone, regardless of their differences, into the education system from an early age, given that the school has a social function, where schooling takes place in space and time, so it is necessary that the people who are served there need to be seen and understood as normal.

In other words, at school, the process of inclusion is based on the *"stimulus-response of learning to complex human accompaniments, especially languages"* (VYGOTSKY 2010), and in order to guarantee this stimulus-response, the teacher's mediation becomes preponderant.

It is at this point that the school assumes its social role. However, in order for this to be realized, some gaps need to be bridged in order to make human rights a reality. Among these are the guarantee of an education based on the necessary adjustments so that, at all levels of education, subjects can be guaranteed the right to be and to be in space, while at the same time being able to do and learn with quality and equity.

However, for this guarantee to be effective, one of the challenges to be resolved lies in the need for continuing training for teachers, as well as how they understand the process of inclusion, so that they can really be in a position to carry out planning aimed at everyone's participation in the development of teaching and learning, teachers must take on the role of mediator to work towards teaching how to do and how to do the teaching-learning process.

Therefore, it is up to the teacher to keep in mind in his pedagogical practice that it is necessary to propose equal treatment for all, but respecting the specificities of individuals, and for this task he needs to understand that there is a need to break with the existing gaps between being and doing pedagogical praxis, because it is necessary to understand that, in order to break these gaps, it is essential to constantly seek training that makes him a research teacher.

Understanding that there is a need to adjust and reorganize its intervention plans frequently makes it truly concerned with individual and collective rights, while at the same time acting to form the exercise of citizenship and human dignity.

The existing ranks, despite the process of inclusion, largely lie in the exclusionary and concentrating model adopted by the country over the centuries, accentuated by the paradigm of globalization, where there is a dualism in education, even though public policies advocate equality for all, while on the one hand we see the objectives of inclusion clearly outlined as a right for all, on the other hand we see that the right to teacher training is presented in a marketing way, given that *"Educational Plans cease to be a right and become a service [....] educational policies have been driven by international organizations [...]* (Ens & Gisi 2010 p. 27).

This justifies, therefore, why the school must take on the role of guaranteeing inclusion, to the extent that it works with its peers to build immediate support, promoting the know-how and the how-to of historically constructed knowledge, with the participation of all as its guiding principle, enabling included students to become active, reflective and singing subjects, demystifying the idea that the teacher is not prepared to deal with the public student of human diversity.

From this perspective, the new education professional's ability to deal with the inclusive public requires the integration of new concepts, skills, attitudes and socio-historical values that are perfected through daily experience guided by action research, since it is from this that the teacher can understand his or her own action in the classroom, while at the same time glimpsing the obstacles and continually seeking to overcome them.

It's important to remember that in school inclusion, the students are more important than the teachers, because they promote action and reaction in the classroom, so it's up to the professionals involved in the process to look for mechanisms to overcome the gaps between being and doing pedagogy for everyone, even if they do so on the basis of continuing education courses.

Professionals must be interested and willing to improve their knowledge and their mediation practices in order to do quality work in education. In such a way, they need to be committed to a teaching and learning technique that is meaningful for everyone involved.

It is worth remembering that, in the new context of education, there is no longer room for the subject who thinks of the act of teaching as being a heterogeneous process, without evaluating the public that is being accommodated at school and/or university, and that makes up a whole diversity, Therefore, the organization of the teacher's pedagogical interventions must take on an emancipatory stance, and this is possible from their training.

Thus, the context of inclusion for human rights makes it possible to raise questions about the organization and/or adaptation and adjustment of curricula, as well as the practices developed in everyday school life. Mizukami (1996, p. 60): "*The teacher is the main mediator between socially constructed knowledge and the students. He is also the source of the models, beliefs, values, concepts and preconceptions, and attitudes that they constitute*".

But when we look at the history of public policies designed to deal with diversity, we are actually thinking about the challenges it presents in terms of multicultural humanism in the context of inclusive education for human rights, we are referring to the objectives of public policies and how they guide the human rights education scenario.

The process of inclusion for human rights must be based on ensuring the right to equality for all, regardless of their conditions, while also taking into account the training of education professionals, because although they are thinking about human otherness, it seems obvious to us that this thinking should also be directed at the subjects who transform this otherness into a Human Right to be in the school space and make this stay a learning moment for all.

Many measures have been taken to solve emergency problems, such as inclusive education, but as far as the training of professionals is concerned, it is disconnected from the context of specificities, since the curricula at all levels of education are organized in a fragmented way and by specific areas.

In view of this, inclusive education takes on the role of understanding the subject, with the aim of emancipating him/herself, and starts to distinguish the limits that exist in the levels of education, in spite of valuing all cultures and creeds in space and time, avoiding old stereotypes that promote the silencing of the existence of one to the detriment of the other and, by over-valuing one and under-valuing the other, the teacher plays a fundamental role in overcoming these ranks.

This is because there are gaps to be overcome, because they show that, in order to transform public schools into inclusive, quality spaces, aimed at valuing social, cultural, physical and emotional differences and meeting the educational needs of all, it is essential to remember that there is a centrality in the relationships between the teacher and the subjects served there, thus breaking down the existing obstacles, making clear the true role of basic education aimed at universalization based on the right for all.

For this to really happen, the discourses must not fade away, but must be perpetuated at all times and in all educational policies. (Mainieri, 2005, p. 7).

> The discussion on inclusive policies usually focuses on the socio-political organization needed to make them viable and the individual rights of the target public. The important advances produced by the democratization of society, greatly leveraged by human rights movements, point to the emergence of the construction of less exclusionary social spaces and alternatives for living together in diversity. A culture's ability to deal with the heterogeneities that make it up has become a kind of criterion for assessing its evolutionary stage, especially in times of fundamentalism and intolerance of all kinds, such as the one we live in now

It is important to emphasize that the reflections presented here refer us to a historiographical analysis of the references that underpinned special education from the perspective of integration; on the contrary, we are also making an analysis to understand how these policies understand the process of training educators, of the concept of disability against the backdrop of intellectual disability and the gaps between knowing and doing in mediation practices based on the development of the concept under the new paradigm in the context of inclusive education.

And from this perspective, when working with human diversity, teachers also need to build their history as educators, as masters of the art of mediating, researching and proposing alternatives that turn teaching into learning for everyone. This is the greatest challenge presented to them in the current socio-historical context, given that they need to analyze and understand all the socio-spatial interrelationships that have been idealized throughout the process of their own training as educators, in order to understand that this is indeed everyone's right in the whole essence of the act of teaching.

Teachers in the context of inclusive education need to be aware that it is possible to make a difference, demystifying the idea that they are not prepared to work with students in inclusive education, because this logic leads to discouragement, which is why they need to understand that problems can be overcome, And overcoming them is the key to putting an end to the discomfort experienced in the face of the new challenge presented to them. In other words, making adjustments to the education and teaching-learning process of the special education student makes this a truly inclusive education.

From this perspective, Foerste (2005, p.25) points out that;

> The problem seems not to have been dealt with satisfactorily with the so-called three hundred hours of compulsory internship in teacher training courses. The curricula have not undergone a significant overhaul, and the dichotomy of specific training versus pedagogical training remains unchanged. The study of issues related to basic education continues to be the exclusive responsibility of pedagogical training, offered by didactic departments or faculties of education. There has been no change in the institutional culture regarding the training of teaching professionals.

Vitallino and Valente apud Cortez (1995, p.96) also complement us;

> [...] at the turn of the 20th century, "the teacher is seen as a transmitter of knowledge, as a technician, as a performer of routines, as a baker. As a subject who makes decisions and solves problems", depending on the conception of school, teaching, knowledge, learning and the theory/practice relationship that underpins the theory behind the metaphor. The 21st century, therefore, is heir to an unresolved discussion that may not have a single answer. (2010, p. 33)

In view of the above, it is necessary to understand that human rights, despite special education in contemporary times, lack a complex vision, rationality and resistance to the inequalities that for centuries have excluded many subjects from the rights to a dignified and participatory education. In other words, society needs to understand that human rights are not just textual declarations, nor are they products of a particular culture.

To better explain this, we refer to the writings of Antonio Sidekum (2002) who, when referring to teacher training processes, highlights the need for them to "find the middle ground to define existential decision-making", in other words, teachers need to understand that, their training cannot be considered ready and finished, the opposite also exists, they need and should have the freedom to dare in their actions of mediation in the classroom, they just need to understand that "their involvement, their posture must always be taken into account" in the intercultural context so present in the various levels of education.

It is necessary to overcome the rangos regarding the systematic and empty abstraction imposed by the linearity of the content, with the necessary adjustments to meet the specificities of the subjects served in each time and space, safeguarding the real circumstances of the people and situated in the western conception of law and the value of identity.

It is important to point out that, when we think about the process of inclusion for human rights, we find in the writings of Antonio Sidekum (2002) a definition of teacher training, which justifies the existence of many gaps that still need to be overcome in order to achieve this and with quality for all, because *"the human being not only feels an existential void, but a being to be fully realized"*.

This seems to us to be an appropriate definition in terms of the void experienced by teachers who define themselves as not having received the necessary training to deal with intercultural and multicultural education, while another group crosses this void and pushes them to want to insert themselves into the context in order to make themselves visible, and to do so they try to be bold in their role of doing and how to do it, while at the same time, even timidly, always trying to make a difference.

However, the problems observed in the process of taking pedagogical action lie in the practice of primary school teachers, who still don't know how to develop interdisciplinary or even transdisciplinary work with other areas of knowledge and if they need to work with differences regardless of physical or cognitive conditions, since every difference requires partnerships to work out fair and differentiated teaching methods that will benefit all students. In this sense, Foerste (2005 p 25) points out that:

> One of the aspects most often raised is the fact that in recent times undergraduate courses have been unable to produce alternatives that satisfactorily meet the demands placed on them by primary school professionals, based on their concrete pedagogical work needs. However, it is worth questioning whether this is a task that academia can accomplish without the collaboration of primary school professionals.

This is complemented by Santos (2004, p.18):

> We are once again returning to the need to ask about the relationship between science and virtue, about the value of the so-called ordinary or vulgar knowledge that we, as individuals or collectives, create and use to make sense of our practices and that science insists on considering irrelevant.

In order to do this, the teacher must overcome the abstract view and also the localist view. To put it more clearly, it is known that it is from social relations that the subject develops, but the teacher cannot remain centered on the idea that it is the environment in which the individual is inserted and in which the "own", value in relation to others, predominates, as being the center of attention and of culture and value in the face of differences.

This type of view generates distortions about rights and therefore proposes a certain type of rationality and a mistaken way of putting them into practice. As mentioned by the Vienna Convention (apud Santos 1997).

> [...] all human rights are universal, interdependent and interrelated. The international community must treat human rights globally, fairly and equitably, on the same basis and with the same emphasis. Taking into account the importance of national and regional particularities, as well as the different historical, cultural and religious backgrounds, it is the duty of states, regardless of their political, economic and cultural systems, to promote and protect all human rights and fundamental freedoms.

In this sense, the treatment given to included people is of the utmost importance when it comes to guaranteeing these rights, also because it is the duty of the state and the family to guarantee and respect the rights of citizens, including the right to protest in situations where the state fails to fulfill its responsibilities, This fact justifies the progress made in public policies for inclusion, guided by many social movements that have emerged over the centuries and resulted in the current laws and guidelines for inclusive education, which legitimize the rights of all, where BAUMANN 2013 p. 43) 43) emphasizes that "universal respect and careful cultivation" are needed.

When we think about the quality and otherness of the EU, we need to think first and foremost about the immediate adjustments that need to be made by education professionals so that this part of the population becomes visible to the whole community, because "if human rights are expressions of values", inclusive education needs to think about the whole and no longer about parts, in order to contemplate the individual and collective in society, and this is extremely important in contemporary society.

The challenges that education from the perspective of inclusion needs to overcome lie in the degree of respectability of the human being and being able to measure this in relation to norms and respect, bearing in mind that there is currently an increase in the disrespect or unpreparedness of structures to receive this section of the population, who need to make themselves visible to the community. This is what BAUMAN (2014) calls *"inhuman behavior, moral blindness. Therefore, it is only through national law or international norms that alternatives must be built to curb human rights violations".*

From this perspective, in order for inclusion to take place, it is well known that human thought is gradually innovating its way of looking at learning how to learn. In this sense, it is possible to find a group of professionals full of perspectives that promote small changes related to human rights and how to make people learn how to learn.

This is because society demands peace, knowledge and cooperation from the whole community, including the conscious search to control conflicts, because teaching learning how to learn requires cooperative work between all those involved in the teaching-learning process.

In view of the above, it is important to emphasize that teachers play a key role in this new context, as they need to take into account all the obstacles faced in carrying out their work in the classroom, bearing in mind that this requires changes in the act of carrying out the learning process, and that this requires knowledge about the target audience, as well as knowledge that leads them to be daring in the art of teaching, always promoting the appropriate curricular adjustments.

It is true that teachers need to make use of all the legal guidelines that establish the need for such didactic-methodological changes, regardless of whether they have been trained in one specific area or another, because the assumptions of public policies establish the need for such changes if the learning process is to be effective.

To justify our writings, we refer to the writings of Novoa (1992, p.16) when he states that teacher training is;

> [...] with the dual task of producing a body of knowledge and a normative system, teachers have an increasingly active (and intense) presence in the educational field: the improvement of pedagogical tools and techniques, the introduction of new teaching methods and the broadening of school curricula make it difficult to exercise teaching as a secondary or accessory activity.

In order to understand the ranks that still exist in relation to the process of inclusion, it is necessary to understand the history of the inclusion of people with disabilities, considering that there are different methodologies for teaching and learning. The history shows us that the people who are the target of inclusion were called to participate in mainstream education, at first, with the aim of a proposal for integration, according to which the subject had to adapt to the school, and then to give birth to the new proposal of inclusion for all.

It is therefore necessary to demystify the meaning and significance of integrating and including, because many are only integrated, but not included, since they are not part of the process of learning to learn. This fact is justified by the lack of adjustment in the immediate curricula that must be proposed by teachers in each area of knowledge.

When thinking about inclusion for human rights, public policies must first of all also take into account human resources in the context of diversity, which must be designed for the plurality found at all levels of education, because the process of inclusion was designed for odd subjects and for this it is necessary to put an end to the linearity of curricula, also putting an end to the constraints imposed by a model of education that no longer fits.

In this respect, it is important that in the training process, the most important thing is to provide professionals with the conditions to re-signify concepts, while at the same time enabling them to understand themselves as agents who produce and carry out learning actions in the context of inclusion for human rights, for which they have taken on the role of training and being trained, here Novoa (1992, p 11) complements us by pointing out that

> We need to recognize the scientific deficiencies and conceptual poverty of current teacher training programs. And to situate our reflection beyond the traditional divides (scientific component versus pedagogical component, theoretical disciplines versus methodological disciplines, etc.), suggesting new ways of thinking about the problem of teacher training.

The process of inclusion for human rights not only takes into account the training of teachers, who must be guided by the needs that trigger global actions aimed at individual and collective conditions, but must also look at the process of making for oneself and for the other, safeguarding the specificities of the group with which the teacher will perform his or her role as an educator for inclusion, this is a reality that presents the needs of groups at all levels of education.

And from any change implemented by the process of pedagogical mediation, based on the immediate adjustment promoted by the teacher, it is possible to observe the unveiling of a new social and cultural climate present in the teacher training process, putting an end to old vices present in training programs for inclusion, as Novoa (1995, p.24) points out.

> [...] the place of education and life history is the ground on which formation is built. For this reason, the practice of education defines the space for all theoretical reflection [...]. However, the analysis of training processes, understood from the perspective of learning and change, cannot be done without explicit reference to the way in which an adult has experienced the concrete situations of their own educational journey.

In view of the above, the training of teachers for the inclusion process is provided for by law, but has systematically ignored personal development, confusing the concept of "training and being trained" to make the invisible visible, since many have not yet assimilated the difference between including and integrating, not understanding that the logic of educational activity does not always coincide with the proper dimensions of training.

In order to overcome this obstacle, it is also necessary to create mechanisms that value and/or create mechanisms to articulate the training and projects of schools, which are considered to be organizations with greater margins of autonomy and decision-making, making them truly inclusive.

When "forgetting what it means to train and be trained for inclusion" occurs, it makes it impossible for training to be based on professional development from the dual perspective of the individual teacher and the teaching collective. It is therefore necessary to value pedagogical knowledge in teacher training for inclusion in order to guarantee human rights, given that this knowledge has become preponderant in terms of the need for this new socio-historical moment in education, where teachers need to be prepared to make the invisible visible, present at all levels of education, based on changes in their training process, giving them a new attitude based on the exchange of experiences.

Portuguese educator Antonio Novoa (1995, p 25), when discussing teacher training, points out that.

> Training is not built through accumulation (of courses, knowledge or techniques), but through critical reflection on practice and the permanent (re)construction of a personal identity. That's why it's so important to invest in the person and give status to the knowledge of experience.

However, for Boaventura Souza Santos (1995), the transformations in the process of training teachers for inclusion must "understand time-space", in other words, the levels of education today encompass situations that mean understanding that socio-spatial relations combine at the same time as they conflict, thus bringing about consistent changes in the act of carrying out the educational process. This is because at the dawn of the 21st century, teachers are being called upon to take a new stance on inclusion, as highlighted by Novoa (2009, p.23).

> At the beginning of the 21st century, teachers have reappeared as irreplaceable elements not only in promoting learning, but also in building inclusive processes that respond to the challenges of diversity and in developing appropriate methods for using new technologies.

In this vein, educators need to bear in mind that their training is essential if they are to become the main social capital for dealing with inclusion at the various levels of education, since they are the actors in the action who, without a shadow of a doubt, welcome learning while taking on the role of making learning how to learn, hence the need for their training to be understood as human and social capital for the new context.

For Bayer (2005), the process of training human resources so that the process of inclusion can take place is a basic condition of giving legitimacy to the foundations of the historical continuity of public education policies, taking into account the guiding principles of the immediate changes needed to make learning how to learn a reality. As far as the teaching-learning process is concerned, during the teacher's training he or she needs to understand the importance of all the conceptual foundations related to the difference between including and integrating, taking them on as a driving force and proposing changes in the didactic-methodological structures to make the teaching-learning process effective for all the plurality that presents itself.

In other words, when we refer to the concept of inclusion, it's because there are people who are outside, excluded, while when we refer to the concept of integration, it's because the subject needs to adapt. So that's the meal we're talking about! In most of the cases we've seen, this is inclusion, where the subject needs to adapt to the conditions and not the other way around as the law states, because inclusive education doesn't just refer to people considered to have disabilities, but follows the principle of education for all, since inclusion is much more than being in the same space, and exchanging experiences, and socializing, and being considered in their differences, and also feeling part of a group, identifying with it.

Including, from this perspective, refers to the constant process of knowledge and reciprocity. However, including does not mean making the other person's learning equal, not dominating them, subjecting them to a way of learning that is not their own, but respecting their difference and freeing them from the bond with which they establish unique, common standards of social coexistence.

Thus, the relationship between human rights from the perspective of inclusive education aimed at overcoming cultural differences in basic education places us on the horizon of affirming dignity and otherness. However, it is necessary to highlight the importance of inclusion from the perspective of social construction, guided by an efficient educational policy.

In order to do this, education professionals need to be trained to deal with human rights and be clear about the objectives of inclusion and integration, because they need to identify, produce and organize immediate educational strategies and resources, taking into account the heterogeneous conditions of the population targeted by inclusive education.

They become the actors capable of expanding the pedagogical mediation game by evaluating the expected results. To do this, they need to know how to make, draw up and execute intervention plans that enable continuous changes in the reaction action process.

Educators then need to understand that their actions must be seen as contributing to improving the quality of teaching in the face of the

For this to happen, they need to be trained and understand the need for planning that respects diversity at all levels of education.

Curricula need to be flexible, methodologies and strategies also need to be differentiated, teaching materials need to allow for the exploration and construction of different and collective axes and adjustments for their mediation proposals, specific assistance needs to respect diversity, and through the use of differentiated resources, teacher training will benefit all the subjects that make up the plurality of teaching levels.

As Freire (1996, p.76) adds,

> The world is not. The world is being. As a curious, intelligent, interfering subjectivity in the objectivity with which I dialectically relate, my role in the world is not only that of someone who observes what is happening, but also that of someone who intervenes as a subject of occurrences, the educator cannot give up the exercise of autonomy, pedagogy centered on ethics, respect for the dignity of the students.

It is important to point out that, based on Freire's writings, respect for human rights demands changes in the way we see and think about human rights education, and this leads society to a movement that alters its behavior in terms of how I see myself and how I see the other, in other words, there is no room for a middle ground: either I accept or I don't accept cultural differences.

Inclusion comes about in a way that is committed to human rights education and that promotes significant changes in the human mentality, since education no longer serves to keep old customs alive, but must promote a new culture of citizenship.

Several studies have highlighted the fact that people develop from their relationships with the environment in which they live, so they can also establish relationships with their peers and develop virtues while shaping their behavior in society.

From this perspective, it is essential to promote human rights education, taking care to ensure that the culture is not passed down from generation to generation. In this sense, it is necessary to improve mediation strategies and public education policies, so that the immediate support proposed by teachers results in quality interference for the people included.

It is worth remembering that the immediate adjustments proposed by teachers to the curriculum are justified because human beings are constantly changing and improving, so human rights education refers to preparing individuals to exercise citizenship.

The importance of continuing education is an important coroborator for implementing real inclusion.

The process of learning about human rights consists of the development of the subject linked to the experience of the value of equality. What's more, it allows for the development of solidarity and the ability to perceive the consequences of the decisions that teachers have to make as mediators in the teaching-learning process. Therefore, the process of training teachers in human rights must be clear: their role is to prepare citizens to avoid the barbarities that violate or omit human rights.

In this context, it is essential for teacher training to be clear that its role is to generate the construction of knowledge and strengthen interpersonal affinities in a more collective way in the school environment. For this reason, it is advisable to discuss all the supports that promote immediate adjustments to curricula aimed at teaching and learning for everyone, regardless of their physical or cognitive conditions.

Moving in the same direction, we realize that teacher training is unquestionable for overcoming the existing ranks in relation to the process of inclusion for human rights, because the right to equal opportunities is present and provided for in the law, from the moment it guarantees only access to the common school, for people with a birth disability or even for people who have not had the same possibility as others to go through the educational process to its full extent, due to problems beyond their control, without however ensuring their permanence.

We then realize that the permanence of the included person depends on several factors, including adjustments to the curriculum, because if they don't find stimuli for learning, they tend to drop out of school as the years go by. To this end, educator and researcher Antonio Novoa (1992) points out that the most important thing in this new context is:

> [...] valuing training paradigms that promote the preparation of reflective teachers, who take responsibility for their own professional development and participate as protagonists in the implementation of educational policies (page 27).

This is because in the process of inclusion, in order to make human rights a reality, teachers need to understand not only themselves, but also the processes of learning how to learn and the personal and professional development of themselves for others. This is why they are considered to have a profession in which the historical subject himself is capable of producing his own professional profile, given that he is the actor in the immediate adjustments to the curricula needed for the target audience of inclusive education.

It's worth remembering that both in the process of inclusion and in teacher training, collective and collaborative practices point to ways of resolving conflicts around concepts and, as a rule, in the articulation and (re)construction of teaching knowledge, starting from the recovery of the practice itself, perfecting and readjusting the methods of mediation in the face of the needs of the new organizational contexts, establishing dialogues with the main actors, in this case the group that should become visible.

From the perspective of teacher training for human development, we realized that there is a need to think about school curricula, because they need to be organized, taking into account new knowledge, and to do so they need to rely on immediate adjustments that are re-elaborations of knowledge in networks of meanings that have senses, logics and techniques. However, in order for it to be built in time and space, there is a need for teachers who are equally trained and committed to dealing with different cultures in the school space.

In this vein, Bobio (2004, p.24) complements us by referring to the role of education and the school, from the perspective of human rights, in guaranteeing inclusive education, supported by the training of teachers as agents of learning and learning to do.

> "The fundamental problem with human rights today is not so much to justify them, but to protect them." Given the history of humanity and its various moments, human rights education has always been necessary and relevant, and

It is the school's role to sensitize everyone to the importance of respecting others, their individuality and differences, becoming a space for citizen education.

From this perspective, the school cannot just be considered a transmitter of linear knowledge that has been historically constructed in an abstract way. Rather, it is the place where the process of learning to learn takes place, with the aim of improving learning and citizen and democratic experiences. Therefore, when we talk about inclusion for human rights, we need to consider human beings/students as social beings, inserted in a social organization, in which the conditions must be ensured for them to develop and live with dignity and equality.

To give an example, it should be emphasized that teacher training for inclusion must be clear about the concept of equality, because not everyone needs to have the same physical, intellectual or psychological characteristics, nor the same habits and customs. In addition, the concept of equality of differences is also related to cultural differences between peoples, because even though they are different people, they are still equal as human beings, presenting the same needs and effective capacities to all.

Delving even further into the history of education policies, we realize that there is a pedagogical emptying when they refer to knowledge by promoting cut-outs that deal with the concept of culture, given that they end up forgetting that both are essential to the student, since it is from the opportunities of knowledge that the student can acquire significant learning for life.

However, when applying the principles of the preambles of the laws and decrees that deal with the rights to equality for all without the proper training of teachers, there is a mistaken precipitation, considering that we want everyone to study under the same conditions and thus reduce the levels of demands for equality and qualification so that they have more and more study of the material, that is, they are integrated, but not included.

In the 21st century, despite the process of inclusion, the educational scene presents many contrasts, differences and inequalities, because the school is still organized in a rigid hierarchical pattern in space and time, Although it can change the way it manages its pedagogical administration, the vast majority still keep their bases organized in grades, classes and bimesters, because they believe this model to be ideal, idolizing conduct, norms and procedures that can no longer deal with the dilemmas and contradictions of today.

As such, the school is an excellent place to guarantee education in spite of human rights. In this sense, we need to reflect on the points of tension that occur in the relationships between all of its actors, which promote an understanding of the concept of differences. In order to do this, teachers must take on the role of making the invisible visible at school. From this perspective, Souza (2006, p.33) says that the school needs to: [...] change the references present in interpersonal relationships, most of which are based on bellicose models that constitute, in everyday life, the continuous expressions of readiness to fight, to convince, to combat, to resist, to counter, to battle, to argue, to contest (Maturana, 2004). We have been brought up in a culture of war to choose a few people as equals and exclude all others who are considered adversaries to my existence. The knowledge of war prevents us from recognizing the legitimacy of the other as similar, even if different[...]they develop in us competitive ways of living together, which vampirize singularities and produce multiple neuroses.

In view of the above, the school and its actors need to think about this new social reality, which is full of weaknesses, and therefore needs to be exposed and reflected upon, so that adjustments can be made to the immediate pedagogical intervention programs, as these should promote connections between the thousands of egocentric islands in the classroom, allowing them to see beyond individuality. However, this ideal will only be achieved when the entire school community understands the meaning and significance of the real concept of inclusion and is actually capable of thinking about a pedagogy for human rights.

It is important to emphasize that, in order for the teaching-learning process to become a reality, immediate adjustments to the curricula promoted by teachers at any level of education are essential. Looking at LDBN 9394/96, we find in article 1º the commitment made to training to guarantee human rights for inclusion, safeguarding their physical, cognitive and cultural conditions.

"the formative processes that develop in family life, in human coexistence, at work, in teaching and research institutes, in social movements and civil society organizations and in cultural manifestations". (BRASIL. 1996)

In other words, the immediate curricular adjustments made by teachers need to take into account the values that are embedded in everyday school life, working on them with conceptual, procedural and attitudinal objectives in each specific area.

For Vygostsky (1984), the process of learning how to learn is a fundamental element in thinking about human rights education, since it relates the student's cognitive development to the social and cultural context in which they are inserted. In other words, it relates the higher mental processes represented by: (thought, language, volitional behavior, conscious attention, voluntary memory, etc.), which have their origins in social processes. In this way, it is not through cognitive development that the subject develops, but through socialization that the development of higher mental processes occurs.

In view of this analysis, the teacher plays the role of mediator and executor of the immediate adjustments necessary to favor the construction/reconstruction of knowledge, of the meanings that are transmitted by the target group of inclusive education, which can occur through the intermediation of reflections and social practices or even through the use of instruments, signs and languages used to interpret the world and make the student as independent as possible (Vygotsky, 1984).

It is the teacher's job to establish connections in order to better mediate scientific concepts and everyday life, based on the principles of human rights, mediating knowledge in a process of discovery, production, exchange and cooperation, thus overcoming the dependence of one on the other.

In view of this, teacher training must take into account the fact that the teacher can no longer be a content teacher, but needs to have a mutual understanding of his or her existence, since he or she has to play several roles alternately, both in the relationship with the student and in his or her pedagogical practice itself.

Moving further in this direction, we realize that teacher training from a human rights perspective requires a more reflective professional, whose role is not just to carry out tasks based on transmitting linear knowledge, but rather a teacher who is able to mediate, to analyze their practice, while at the same time being able to make decisions regarding immediate curricular adjustments, adapting them to the specific context in which they take place, and who is also able to corroborate with their colleagues and other professionals so that inclusion really does take place.

Therefore, it is also important to take into account a coherent training model so that they can propose adjustments that justify their role in the act of learning to learn, since knowledge is the result of reflection and action in the classroom, where mediation is no longer personal to one person but becomes part of the common baggage of the whole.

In other words, the teacher learns to the extent that the obstacle puts him to the test, confronting his idea of the teaching-learning process, so he starts to promote adjustments that are designed to develop learning to learn, based on his reflections that are not linked to the instructions for use that come from the curriculum of the common national curriculum.

This is because teaching and learning, despite the process of inclusion for human rights, goes against the logic of linearity in which the two have been separated for centuries, given that curricula have always been exclusively concerned with teaching to the detriment of learning. We understand that the two need to go hand in hand, as they both complement human rights.

Thus, the teacher training process must take into account that the misunderstandings surrounding the traditional curriculum must be dispelled, i.e. we are not referring here to the fact that the common core curriculum cannot be taken into account; on the contrary, it needs to be adjusted to the immediate reality necessary for learning to learn to take place.

This is because, for students who are the target of inclusive education, traditional teaching in the form of content is vague and uninteresting. However, when the teacher makes adjustments that show some equivalence with their proximal zone, the process of mediation becomes more interesting and, as a result, brings them closer to learning how to learn.

In this way, the more the teacher is involved in the immediate curriculum adjustments, the better their practice and commitment to the process of learning to learn will be and, consequently, to the realization of inclusion, which will result in the guarantee of human rights for all, regardless of the physical, cognitive and cultural conditions of this or that group.

To put it more succinctly, the teacher needs to create an environment where learning is of interest to the group he or she is working with. To do this, he or she needs to look for resources that give meaning and significance to his or her and the student's ideas, so that they can construct meaningful answers to the problems that arise during the course of the lesson.

What's more, teachers need to be attentive and committed to their attitudes in the classroom, because they depend on whether they include or integrate students, and know how to make the most of their students' abilities, always bearing in mind that the success of learning how to learn will depend on the flexibility of their immediate curricular adjustments, because the group may show concerns that lead to learning progress or not, depending on the educator's pedagogical approach.

In short, the training of teachers in human rights must take into account the reality of their surroundings, in this case the classroom, and be guided by their concrete experience and individual needs, be they their own and/or those of their students, because these (differences) are not taken into account by the official curricula, and propose adjustments that will result in the processes of learning to learn, for themselves and for others.

Considering that the subject's integral formation is based on learning, and that this learning needs to be significant, but for this to happen, mediation needs to capture the attention of the whole group, which needs to become visible in the face of school diversity. But for this to actually happen, the main aspects to be considered are the resources that will guide the immediate curricular adjustments made by teachers.

In other words, in order for learning to learn to reach the desired levels, mediation proposals need to be appropriate to reduce the distance between what the student knows and wants to learn, and what the teacher wants to teach, because if the student finds it difficult, the mediation proposal between knowing and doing will be null and void, since the group will feel demotivated by having to learn what they already know or what is abstract to their conditions.

The teacher needs to take into account that every subject always knows something about what makes up the proposed mediation, so he or she needs to propose adjustments that suit everyone's characteristics, thus making teaching inclusive to the extent that it makes visible the group that for centuries has been on the margins of the teaching-learning process.

From this perspective, teachers need to take into account that learning is an educational act that results from reaction, but they also need to be clear that the immediate adjustments made to curricula must be based on the principle that students are not a kind of "Tabula rasa"; on the contrary, they must respect the rhythm of each one, or they will remain in the old vices of linear curricula centered on subjects in drawers.

Vygostky (2010) states that if we change the instruments of thought that the child (student, my emphasis) uses, his mind will be radically different. Therefore, the role of the teacher in making immediate adjustments today is fundamental, given that he or she can make use of an endless range of instruments that can operate on the student, including configuration in different ways, and this results in learning to learn as the proactive principle of teaching and learning, with the zone of proximal development as the driving force.

In other words, the relationships that the teacher will establish with the abstract content are not exactly direct with the student's lived reality, but through meaningful means and materials that represent reality and thus bring it closer and/or facilitate access to or understanding of the content based on observation and can also occur from the research of this reality depending on the level of education in which the student is inserted, safeguarding their physical and cognitive conditions.

When we talk about the process of inclusion for human rights, it is important to point out that there have been significant advances in terms of the development of the individual who is already in the school environment, but there are still areas that need to be improved in terms of the training of human resources to work with diversity, since the training is designed for one area of knowledge, but inclusion is dynamic and affects all levels of education.

Mantoan (2009) points out that the problem of inclusion is a broad issue, which is why it is necessary to think of a school model that offers much more than just assistance to students with disabilities. In other words, a reflective reading of the current model shows that there is an exclusive preoccupation with training teachers according to the existing school model, It is not being taken into account that there is an intense diversity in the school that cries out for recognition and in this sense it is necessary to understand the new meaning of what this training is for everyone, but the school environment today is very restrictive, and in itself challenging, so it is up to the teacher to know how to intervene and know how to mediate knowledge in the face of this new school scenario.

Despite all the progress that inclusion has made towards the realization of human rights over the last few decades, there is still a lot to be improved, because it is necessary to break away from the idea that the school is not prepared to deal with diversity; on the contrary, if it is in the school that this diversity is most visible, the clashes and discussions can take shape, and this is challenging, The school, as well as its teachers and managers, need to understand that diversity must be part of these discussions, because it is they who strengthen the stage of the struggles for the recognition of human rights and from them break with any and all opposing opinions making the school environment more homogeneous and welcoming.

However, it is also known that the teacher's training is preponderant in this new perspective, given that by training the teacher becomes the main ingredient in making the school a more welcoming space, making diversity just another component to enrich their pedagogical practice, because they will know how to mediate and recognize everyone, establishing the importance of the value of each one and that together everyone learns.

4 BIBLIOGRAPHICAL REFERENCES

BRAZIL. LAW No. 12796 of April 4, 2013. Provisions on LDBN 9394/96 - highlighting curricular adjustments to meet special needs, global development disorders and high skills or giftedness. Available at :http://www.planalto.gov.br/ccivil03/ ato2011-2014/2013/lei/l12796.htm- acesso em 18.01.2017

BRAZIL. Ministry of Education. TECHNICAL NOTE - SEESP/GAB/N⁰ 9/2010 of April 9, 2010. Brasilia, 2010.

Brasilia: Ministry of Education, Special Education Secretariat, 2005.
Political and Legal Milestones of Special Education from the Perspective of Inclusive Education, 2010.

BRASIL.Resolugao CNE/CEB 04 de 02 de outubro de 2009. Operational Guidelines for Specialized Educational Assistance in Basic Education, Special Education modality. 2009.

BRASIL. National Policy for Special Education from the Perspective of Inclusive Education. MEC. Brasilia, 2008a. Available at:http://portal.mec.gov.br/seesp/arquivos/pdf/politica.pdf.

BRAZIL. Projeto Escola Viva: guaranteeing access and permanence for all students at school: students' special educational needs. Brasilia: Ministry of Education, Department of Special Education - Historical Overview, v 1, 2005.

BRAZIL. Ministry of Education. National Education Council. National Guidelines for Special Education in Basic Education. Resolution 02/2001. MEC/ SEESP, Brasilia, 2001.

BRAZIL. MEC/SEB/SEESP. National curricular parameters - curricular adaptations: teaching strategies for the education of students with special educational needs. Brasilia: 1998b.

BRAZIL. Children with special educational needs, educational policy and teacher training: generalists or specialists? Revista Brasileira de Educagao Especial, Piracicaba: UNIMEP, v. 3, n. 5, p. 7-25, 1999.

BRAZIL. 1988 Constitution of the Federative Republic of Brazil. Available at:<http://www.planalto.gov.br/ccivil_03/constituicao/constituicao.htm>.

Accessed on: 15.01.2017.

BRAZIL. National Education Guidelines and Bases Law - LDB: Law No. 9394/96, which establishes the guidelines and bases of national education.

BAUMAN Zygmunt, Cegueira Moral: A perda da sensibilidade na modernidade liquida / Zymunt Bauman, Leonidas Donskis; tradugao Carlos Alberto Medeiros - 1.ed.-Rio de Janeiro: Zahar, 2014.

BAUMAN,Zygmunt. Aculturanoano mundo liquido moderno; tradugao Carlos Alberto Medeiros.-1. Ed.-Rio de Janeiro: Zahar, 2013.

BEYER, H. O. Inclusão e avaliagao na escola: de alunos com necessidades educacionais especiais. Porto Alegre: Mediagao, 2005

BOBBIO, Norberto. The Age of Rights. Translated by Carlos Nelson Coutinho. Introduction by Celso Lafer. Rio de Janeiro: Elsevier, 2004.

dimensoes-tecnicas-e-politicas-em-discussao.pdf>. Accessed on: October 11, 2013.

BONAVIDES, Paulo. Course in constitutional law. 9. ed. Sao Paulo: Malheiros, 2000.

CARBONARI, Paulo Cesar Human Rights: pedagogical suggestions. Passo Fundo: IFIBE, 2010.

CARVALHO, Rosita Edler. Special education policies. Revista Intercontinental de Psicologia y Educacion, enero-junio, v. 10, n.001,2008.

ENS, R. T.; GISI, M. L.; EYNG, A. M. The teaching profession in question: tensions and challenges. In: ENS, R. T.; BEHRENS, M. A. (Org.). Teacher training: professionalism, research and school culture. Curitiba: Champagnat, 2010. p. 4374.

FOERSTE, Erineu. Partnership in Teacher Training. Ed. Cortez 2005, Sao Paulo

FREIRE, Paulo. Pedagogy of autonomy: knowledge necessary for educational practice. Sao Paulo: Paz e Terra, 1996.

HEREDERO, E. S. Necessidades Educativas Especiales y Adaptaciones Curriculares. Marilia: Unesp, FFC, Department of Special Education, 1999.

HOBSBAWM, Eric. The Age of Extremes: The Short Twentieth Century - 1914 - 1991 - Sao Paulo, Cia das Letras.

JANNUZZI, Gilberta, Martino de. The Education of the Disabled in Brazil From the Beginnings to the 21st Century. Autores & Associados. Campinas SP. 3 Ed. 2012

MAGENDZO, A. (Org.) Educacion en Derechos Humanos: apuntes para una nueva practica Chile: Corporacion Nacional de Reparacion y Reconciliacion and PIIE, 1994.

MAGALHAES, Rita de Cassia Barbosa Paiva. Curriculum in special education: technical and political dimensions under discussion. In: GONQALVES, Eniceia Mendes; ALMEIDA, Maria Amelia. (Orgs.). Pedagogical dimensions in school inclusion practices. Marilia: ABPEE, v. 2, p. 491-507, 2012. Available at: <http://www.ppgees.ufscar.br/capitulo-31-curriculo-emeducacao-especial-dimensoes-tecnicas-e-politicas-em-discussao.pdf>. Accessed on: 11 Jan 2017.

MAINIERI, Paulon, Simone. Document supporting the inclusion policy. Brasilia: Ministry of Education, Special Education Secretariat, 2005.

MANTOAN, Maria Teresa Egler; PRIETO, Rosangela Gavioli. School Inclusion. Sao Paulo: Sammus, 2006.

Overcoming barriers and moving forward in school inclusion. In: CORREA, Rosa Maria (Org.). Advances and challenges in building an inclusive society. Belo Horizonte: Inclusive Society/PUC-MG, 2008.

MAZZOTTA, M. J. S. Trabalho docente e formacao de professores de educagao especial. Sao Paulo: EPU, 2003.

, Special Education in Brazil. Histories and Public Policies. Sao Paulo. Cortez, 2001

MICHELLS, Maria. H & GARCIA, Rosalba M. C. A Organização Curricular na Articulação Entre Serviço Especializado e Classe Comum: Um Modelo Inclusivo? (Org) KASSAR. Monica de Carvalho M. Dialogue with Diversity. Challenges for the Training of Educators in Contemporary Times. Mercado das Letras. 2010. SP.

MIZUKAMI, M. G. N. **Ensino**: As abordagens do processo. Sao Paulo: EPU, 1996.

MELLO, G.N. Politicas Publicas de Educagao. Advanced Studies. Sao Paulo: USP, 1991 (Serie educagao para a cidadania, n1).

SANTOS, Boaventura de Sousa. Uma cartografia simbolica das representações sociais: prolegomenos e uma concepción pos-moderna do direito. Revista Critica de Ciencias Sociais, n. 28, 1988, p.164-187.

SANTOS, Boaventura de Sousa. For a multicultural conception of human rights. Coimbra - Revista Critica de Ciencias Sociais, No. 48, June 1997.

SIDEKUM, Antonio. Fundamental Rights: Human Dignity. Nova Petropolis: Nova Harmonia, 2002.

SOUSA, A. M. B. Biocentric education: weaving an understanding. Revista Pensamento Biocentrico,n. 5,jan./jul.2006. Available at: http://www.pensamentobiocentrico.com.br/content/ed05 art01 .php http:/accessed on 18.01.2017

SANTOS, B. de S. (Org.). Prudent knowledge for a decent life: A discourse on the sciences revisited. Sao Paulo: Cortez, 2004.

SOUZA, Santos Boaventura de. O discurso e o poder: ensaio sobre a sociologia da retorica juridical. Porto Alegre: Sergio Antonio Fabris, 1998.

UNESCO. Salamanca declaration and line of action on special educational needs. Salamanca, 1994.

VITALIANO, Celia Regina & VALENTE Silza Maria Pasella. The Training of Reflective Teachers as a Necessary Condition for the Inclusion of Students with Special Educational Needs. In VITALIANO (ORG) Teacher Training for the Inclusion of Students with Special Educational Needs. Eduel. 2010. Londrina. PR.

VYGOTSKY, L. S. The social formation of the mind. Sao Paulo: Martins Fontes, 2010.

. Language, development and learning. 2 ed. Sao Paulo: Icone, 2010.

WALLON, Henri. The psychological evolution of the child. Martins Fontes, Sao Paulo 2010.

yes **I want** morebooks!

Buy your books fast and straightforward online - at one of world's fastest growing online book stores! Environmentally sound due to Print-on-Demand technologies.

Buy your books online at
www.morebooks.shop

Kaufen Sie Ihre Bücher schnell und unkompliziert online – auf einer der am schnellsten wachsenden Buchhandelsplattformen weltweit! Dank Print-On-Demand umwelt- und ressourcenschonend produzi ert.

Bücher schneller online kaufen
www.morebooks.shop

info@omniscriptum.com
www.omniscriptum.com

Printed by Books on Demand GmbH, Norderstedt / Germany